ISBN 979-8-9922496-9-9

Please address inquiries to:
boycepearson@sbcglobal.net

WEALTH AND WISDOM

Exploring Money through the Bible

By Boyce N. Pearson

To my wife, family members, and true friends

— CONTENTS —

Introduction: A brief note about this book iv

Chapter 1: Wealth and Prosperity 1

Chapter 2: The Dangers of Money 12

Chapter 3: Generosity and Giving 18

Chapter 4: Poverty and Social Justice. 22

Chapter 5: Steward and Management. 37

Chapter 6: Trust, Contentment, and Providence. 45

Chapter 7: Application to Modern Life. 51

Conclusion: A Call to Action 53

Appendix 55

Bibliography 57

About the Author 60

— INTRODUCTION —

Exploring biblical perspectives on wealth, poverty, stewardship, and generosity will provide profound insights into how individuals should approach their financial lives and interact with each other in society.

1. **Wealth:** The Bible acknowledges that wealth itself is not inherently sinful, but it warns against the love of money, which is often referred to as the root of all evil (1 Timothy 6:10). Instead wealth is seen as a gift from God to be stewarded responsibly (Deuteronomy 8:18). It emphasizes the importance of not placing one's trust solely in riches but in God (Proverbs 11:28) and warns against the dangers of greed and hoarding (Luke 12:15).

2. **Poverty:** The Bible is replete with teachings on caring for the poor and marginalized. It emphasizes God's concern for the poor and calls upon believers to show compassion and generosity towards them (Proverbs 19:17, Matthew 25:35-40). Poverty is not glorified but seen as a condition to be alleviated through acts of justice and mercy (Isaiah 58: 6-7).

3. **Stewardship:** The concept of stewardship is central to biblical teachings on wealth and resources. Stewardship emphasizes that everything belongs to God and humans are merely caretakers or managers of God's possessions (Psalm 24:1). It calls for responsible management and accountability for how resources are used whether they are finances, time, talents, or the environment. This includes wise

investing, budgeting, and planning for the future (Matthew 25:14-30).

4. **Generosity:** Generosity is a recurring theme in the Bible, with numerous exhortations to give freely and cheerfully (2 Corinthians 9:7). It teaches that generosity is not only about material giving but also encompasses acts of kindness, forgiveness, and love. The biblical model of generosity often has the power to shape our beliefs and principles over time. By aligning our financial choices with our deepest convictions and aspirations, we can lead more fulfilling and purpose-driven lives, making a positive impact on ourselves and the world around us.

— Importance of Understanding Money in a Spiritual Context —

Financial decisions are deeply intertwined with our beliefs and values, often serving as a tangible expression of what we prioritize and hold dear. Whether consciously or unconsciously, our faith and values play a significant role in shaping how we manage money and make financial choices.

First and foremost, faith can influence financial decisions through the principles and teachings it imparts. Many religious traditions have specific guidelines regarding wealth, charity, and stewardship. For example, in Christianity, the Bible teaches principles such as stewardship, generosity, and avoiding the love of money. These teachings can directly impact how adherents approach earning, spending, saving, and giving. Similarly, in Islam, there are specific guidelines on earning halal (permissible) income, avoiding riba (interest), and practicing zakat (mandatory charity).

These principles guide Muslims in their financial dealings and decisions.

Values, whether derived from religious teachings or personal convictions, also shape financial decisions. For instance, someone who values environmental sustainability may prioritize investing in eco-friendly companies or purchasing energy-efficient appliances, even if it comes at a higher cost. Similarly, someone who values education may be willing to invest more in their children's schooling, even if it means making sacrifices in other areas of their budget.

Moreover, financial decisions can reflect our priorities and what we hold as important in life. For some, this might mean prioritizing experiences over material possessions, leading to decisions such as budgeting for travel or spending on luxury items. For others, it could mean prioritizing financial security for their family, leading to decisions like purchasing life insurance or saving for retirement diligently.

Conversely, our financial decisions can also shape our faith and values over time. For example, consistently practicing generosity by giving to charitable causes can deepen one's sense of compassion and empathy, reinforcing values of altruism and social responsibility. Similarly, making ethical investment choices can align with one's values and contribute to positive social or environmental change reinforcing those values in the process.

However, it's essential to recognize that financial decisions are not solely determined by faith and values. Practical considerations such as income level, financial obligations, and economic circumstances, also play a significant role.

Sometimes, individuals may face tensions between their faith/values and financial realities, requiring thoughtful discernment and compromise.

In conclusion, financial decisions are a reflection of our faith values and priorities, and they, in turn, have the power to shape our beliefs and principles over time. By aligning our financial choices with our deepest convictions and aspirations, we can lead more fulfilling and purpose-driven lives, making a positive impact on ourselves and the world we live in.

Scripture quotations are taken from the Holy Bible, New King James Version.

CHAPTER ONE

— Wealth and Prosperity —

Proverbs 10:22 states, "The blessing of the Lord brings wealth, without painful toil for it. "This verse encapsulates a profound biblical perspective on the nature of wealth and prosperity.

From a biblical standpoint, the concept of blessing is deeply rooted in the idea of divine favor and provision. Throughout the Bible, blessings are seen as gifts from God, given out of His abundant grace and love for His people. These blessings can manifest in various forms, including material prosperity, health, relationships, and spiritual growth.

Proverbs 10:22 suggests that true wealth and prosperity ultimately come from God's blessing. This implies that God's favor is the ultimate source of prosperity, rather than solely human effort or labor. While hard work and diligence are important virtues emphasized throughout the Bible, Proverbs 6:6-11 highlights that God's blessing can transcend human effort and bring about prosperity in ways that are unexpected and beyond our abilities.

Furthermore, the phrase "without painful toil for it" does not necessarily imply that there is no effort involved in acquiring wealth. Instead, it suggests that the source of wealth is not solely dependent on human toil or laborious striving. While hard work is valued, the ultimate source of prosperity is God's blessing, which can bring about abundance in a manner that surpasses human striving alone.

This verse also underscores the importance of recognizing and acknowledging God's role as the provider of all good things. It encourages humility and dependence on God rather than placing undue trust in one's abilities or resources. It reminds believers that true wealth is not solely measured by material possessions but by the presence of God's blessing in their lives.

Overall, Proverbs 10:22 teaches believers to trust in God's provision and blessing, recognizing that true wealth and prosperity ultimately come from Him. It encourages a perspective of gratitude, humility, and reliance on God's faithfulness, even in the pursuit of material abundance.

Deuteronomy 8:18 is a powerful reminder of the divine source of wealth and prosperity. The verse says, "But remember the Lord your God, for it is he who gives you the ability to produce wealth." This verse is part of Moses' exhortation to the Israelites as they were about to enter the Promised Land, reminding them of God's faithfulness and provision throughout their journey.

At its core, Deuteronomy 8:18 emphasizes several key biblical principles regarding wealth:

1. **God as the Source of Blessing:** The verse underscores the foundational belief that God is the ultimate source of all blessings, including wealth and prosperity. It serves as a reminder to acknowledge and honor God as the giver of every good gift (James 1:17), recognizing that all our abilities, opportunities, and resources come from Him.

2. **Human Responsibility and Partnership with God:** While God is acknowledged as the source of wealth, the verse also highlights the role of human agency in producing wealth. God gives the Israelites the ability to produce wealth indicating a partnership between divine provision and human effort. This aligns with other biblical teachings that emphasize the value of hard work, diligence, and wise stewardship (Proverbs 10:4; 13:11).

Gratitude and Remembrance: Remembering the Lord and His faithfulness is a recurring theme in Deuteronomy, and it is particularly emphasized in verse 18. Acknowledging God as the source of wealth cultivates gratitude and humility among His people. By remembering God's provision in the past and recognizing His ongoing blessings in the present, believers are reminded of their dependence on Him and are motivated to live in faithful obedience to His covenant.

Fulfillment of Promises: The verse also highlights the fulfillment of God's promises to His people. The ability to produce wealth serves as a tangible manifestation of God's faithfulness in fulfilling His covenant commitments to Israel and their ancestors. This reinforces the trustworthiness of God's word and His commitment to bless His people abundantly, according to His covenant promises.

These verses, particularly Deuteronomy 8:18, speak profoundly to the concept of divine blessing and the recognition that our abilities and opportunities come from God. They offer a reflection on the relationship between God's provision and human responsibility, highlighting several key points:

Divine Blessing as the Source of Provision: The verses underscore the foundational belief that all blessings, including abilities, opportunities, and wealth, originate from God. This perspective acknowledges God's sovereignty and generosity as the ultimate source of every good gift in our lives (James 1:17). It encourages humility and gratitude, recognizing that our talents and opportunities are not the result of our merit or efforts alone but are gifts bestowed upon us by a gracious and loving God.

Human Cooperation with God's Provision: While God is acknowledged as the giver of abilities and opportunities, there is also an emphasis on human cooperation and responsibility. God grants the Israelites the ability to produce wealth, but they are called to actively participate in the process through their labor and stewardship. This partnership between divine provision and human effort reflects a broader biblical theme of collaboration between God and humanity in fulfilling His purposes on earth.

Gratitude and Recognition of God's Faithfulness: The verses urge believers to remember and reflect on God's faithfulness and provision in their lives. By recalling God's past acts of provision, protection, and guidance, believers cultivate gratitude and trust in His ongoing care. This remembrance serves as a safeguard against pride, self-reliance, and forgetfulness of God's goodness amidst prosperity.

Stewardship and Accountability: Implicit in the concept of divine blessing is the call to responsible stewardship. Believers are entrusted with God-given abilities and opportunities, which they are accountable for using wisely and ethically. This entails utilizing one's talents and resources for God's purposes, contributing to the well-being of others, and advancing His kingdom on earth. Stewardship involves both the wise management of wealth and the responsible exercise of influence and leadership in various spheres of life.

In summary, these verses reflect a holistic understanding of divine blessing and the recognition that abilities and opportunities ultimately come from God. They encourage believers to acknowledge God's sovereignty, cooperate with His provision, cultivate gratitude for His faithfulness, and exercise responsible stewardship in all aspects of life. By embracing these principles, believers can live lives marked by humility, gratitude, and faithful obedience to God's will.

— The Role of Wealth in the Bible —

In both Testaments, wealth was viewed and used in various ways, reflecting the social, cultural, and religious contexts of the time. However, there are also notable differences in how wealth is portrayed and addressed between the two testaments.

Old Testament Perspectives on Wealth:

1. **Blessing and Provision:** In the Old Testament, wealth was often seen as a sign of God's blessing and provision. Prosperity, including material abundance, was viewed as a reward for obedience to God's commandments (Deuteronomy 28:1-14). Conversely, poverty and lack were sometimes interpreted as signs of divine disfavor or judgment (Deuteronomy 28:15-68).

2. **Stewardship and Justice:** The Old Testament emphasizes principles of stewardship and social justice regarding wealth. God commanded the Israelites to care for the poor, widows, orphans, and strangers, demonstrating compassion and generosity (Deuteronomy 15:7-11, Proverbs 22:9). The prophets frequently condemned the exploitation of the poor and the accumulation of wealth through unjust means (Isaiah 5:8, Amos 5:11-12).

3. **Material Prosperity and Spiritual Danger:** While wealth was considered a blessing, the Old Testament also warned against the dangers of wealth and the love of money. The pursuit of riches could lead to pride, greed, and a neglect of spiritual priorities (Proverbs 11:28, Ecclesiastes 5:10-15).

New Testament Perspectives on Wealth:

1. **Spiritual Values Over Material Wealth:** In the New Testament, Jesus and the apostles often emphasized spiritual values over material wealth. Jesus taught that true riches are found in a relationship with God and the treasures of heaven, rather than earthly possessions (Matthew 6:19-21, Luke 12:15). He challenged the rich to sell their possessions, give to the poor, and follow Him (Matthew 19:21, Luke 18:22).

2. **Generosity and Sacrifice:** The New Testament highlights the importance of generosity, sacrificial giving, and sharing resources with others. Jesus praised the widow who gave her last two coins as an example of true generosity (Mark 12:41-44). The

early Christian community practiced radical sharing and communal living, selling their possessions to meet the needs of others (Acts 2:44-45; 4:32-35).

3. **Warning Against the Love of Money:** The New Testament warns against the love of money and the pursuit of wealth as idols that can lead to spiritual harm (1 Timothy 6:9-10). Paul advises believers to be content with what they have and to pursue godliness rather than pursuing riches (1 Timothy 6:6-8).

Both Testaments offer perspectives on wealth that emphasize the importance of stewardship, justice, compassion, and spiritual values. While the Old Testament often portrays wealth as a sign of God's blessing and provision with an emphasis on social responsibility, the New Testament emphasizes spiritual priorities, sacrificial giving, and warning against the dangers of wealth and materialism.

Ecclesiastes 5:10 provides a profound reflection on the vanity associated with the love of money and its potential downfall for humanity. The verse reads, "Whoever loves money never has enough; Whoever loves wealth is never satisfied with their income. This too is meaningless."

1. **Insatiable Desire:** One of the key insights from this verse is the insatiable nature of the love of money. The pursuit of wealth is depicted as a never-ending cycle where individuals are constantly striving for more, yet they never find true satisfaction or contentment. This insatiable desire for wealth can lead to a relentless pursuit of material possessions and financial gain, often at the expense of other aspects of life such as relationships, health, and spiritual well-being.

7

2. **Meaninglessness and Vanity:** Ecclesiastes often explores the theme of vanity or meaninglessness in human endeavors, and the pursuit of wealth is no exception. The verse suggests that the love of money ultimately leads to a futile and empty existence, devoid of true purpose or fulfillment. Despite accumulating wealth, those who love money find themselves trapped in a never-ending quest for more, unable to find lasting satisfaction or meaning in their pursuits.

3. **Discontentment and Disillusionment:** Another implication of the love of money highlighted in this verse is the pervasive sense of discontentment and disillusionment it breeds. Rather than bringing happiness or fulfillment, the relentless pursuit of wealth often leads to disappointment and disillusionment as individuals realize that material possessions alone cannot satisfy the deepest longings of the human heart. This constant craving for more can also lead to anxiety, stress, and a lack of peace in one's life.

4. **Spiritual and Moral Dangers:** Beyond its consequences, the love of money can also have broader spiritual and moral implications. It can lead individuals to prioritize self-interest over the well-being of others, to engage in unethical or immoral behavior to acquire wealth, and to neglect spiritual values and principles in favor of material gain. In this way, the love of money can become a stumbling block to living a life of integrity, compassion, and spiritual fulfillment.

In summary, Ecclesiastes 5:10 offers a sobering reflection on the vanity associated with the love of money and its potential downfall for humanity. It warns against the insatiable desire for wealth, the emptiness of material pursuits, and the spiritual and moral dangers inherent in the relentless pursuit of financial gain. Instead, it encourages individuals to seek true meaning and fulfillment in life through relationships, virtue, and a deeper connection with the divine.

1. **King Solomon:**

   - King Solomon, known for his wisdom, offers insights into the purpose of wealth in the books of Proverbs and Ecclesiastes.

   - In Proverbs, Solomon emphasizes the importance of diligence, hard work, and wise stewardship in acquiring wealth (Proverbs 10:4; 13:11).

   - In Ecclesiastes, Solomon reflects on the vanity and transience of material pursuits, cautioning against placing too much emphasis on wealth and earthly possessions (Ecclesiastes 5:10; 5:15-17).

   - Solomon ultimately concludes that true meaning and fulfillment are found in fearing God and keeping His commandments, rather than in the accumulation of wealth (Ecclesiastes 12:13).

2. **Job:**

   - The story of Job provides a nuanced perspective on the purpose of wealth and the meaning of prosperity.

9

- Job, a righteous man, experiences immense suffering and loss, including the loss of his wealth and possessions.

- Through his trials, Job wrestles with questions of the purpose of wealth and the nature of God's providence.

- Ultimately, Job learns to trust in God's sovereignty and goodness recognizing that true wealth lies in his relationship with God, rather than in material possessions (Job 1:21; 42:10-17).

3. **Jesus Christ:**

- Jesus offers profound teachings on the purpose of wealth and how it should be viewed in light of the kingdom of God.

- Jesus warns against the love of money and the pursuit of wealth as idols that can lead to spiritual harm (Matthew 6:24, Luke 12:15).

- He teaches that true riches are found in a relationship with God and the treasures of heaven rather than in earthly possessions (Matthew 6:19-21).

- Jesus emphasizes the importance of generosity, sacrificial giving, and using wealth to help the poor and marginalized (Matthew 25:35-40, Luke 12:33-34).

4. **Paul:**

- The apostle Paul provides practical guidance on

the purpose of wealth and how it should be viewed within the Christian community.

- Paul warns against the dangers of the love of money and encourages believers to be content with what they have (1 Timothy 6:6-10, Philippians 4:11-13).

- He emphasizes the importance of generosity, cheerful giving, and using wealth to advance the kingdom of God and support the needs of others (2 Corinthians 9:6-8, 1 Timothy 6:17-19).

In summary, the purpose of wealth and how it should be viewed, according to different biblical characters and authors, encompasses a range of perspectives, including diligence, stewardship, contentment, generosity, and prioritizing spiritual values over material possessions.
Ultimately, the Bible teaches that true wealth is found in a relationship with God and in using our resources to glorify Him and bless others.

CHAPTER TWO

— The Dangers of Money —

The passage from 1 Timothy 6:10 famously states, "For the love of money is a root of all kinds of evil. Some people eager for money have wandered from the faith and pierced themselves with many griefs." This verse is often quoted to highlight the dangers of prioritizing wealth and material gain above all else.

At its core, this verse warns against the unhealthy obsession with money. It's not money itself that is condemned, but rather the love of it, the relentless pursuit of it at the expense of other values. When people prioritize wealth above all else, they can easily stray from moral and ethical paths. Their actions may become driven solely by the desire for financial gain, leading them to engage in deceitful, unethical, or even criminal behavior.

"A root of all kinds of evil" suggests that many societal ills can be traced back to the love of money. This isn't to say that every evil act is directly motivated by greed, but rather that greed can be a significant contributing factor to many wrongdoings. For instance, corruption in government exploitation of workers, environmental degradation, and even interpersonal conflicts can often be tied, at least in part, to the pursuit of wealth at any cost.

Moreover, the verse warns that this love of money can lead individuals away from their faith and spiritual well-being. When money becomes the primary focus of one's life, it can overshadow values such as compassion, generosity, and integrity. This shift in priorities can have profound spiritual and emotional consequences, leaving individuals feeling empty, unfulfilled, and disconnected from deeper aspects of life.

In essence, 1 Timothy 6:10 serves as a cautionary reminder about the potential pitfalls of prioritizing the pursuit of wealth above all else. It invites reflection on the deeper values and priorities that guide our lives and encourages a more balanced and conscientious approach to matters of money and material gain.

In Luke 12-15, Jesus delivers a powerful warning against greed with the statement, "Take care, and be on your guard against all covetousness, for one's life does not consist in the abundance of his possessions." This verse is part of a larger passage where Jesus addresses a crowd teaching them about the dangers of placing too much emphasis on material wealth and possessions.

At the heart of this warning is the recognition that true fulfillment and purpose in life cannot be found in material wealth alone. Jesus urges his followers to be vigilant and cautious, guarding against the temptation to constantly desire more and accumulate possessions. He emphasizes that life's richness isn't measured by the abundance of possessions one owns but rather by the quality of their relationships, character and spiritual well-being.

Greed or covetousness is depicted here as a pervasive danger that can subtly infiltrate every aspect of life. It's not just about the desire for money or material possessions but extends to an insatiable craving for more—more wealth, more power, more status. This insatiable desire can lead to a never-ending cycle of discontentment as one constantly strives for more without ever finding true satisfaction.

Furthermore, Jesus' warning against greed underscores the ethical and moral implications of such a mindset. When individuals prioritize their desires for wealth and possessions above all else, they may neglect the needs of others, exploit those who are less fortunate or engage in dishonest and unethical behavior to satisfy their desires.

Ultimately this verse encourages self-reflection and reevaluation of priorities. It challenges individuals to seek fulfillment and meaning in things beyond material wealth and to cultivate virtues such as generosity, contentment, and compassion. By recognizing the limitations of material possessions and guarding against the grip of greed one can pursue a more fulfilling and spiritually enriching life in alignment with the teachings of Jesus.

1. **Short-Term Gains vs. Long-Term Values:**

- **Short-Term Gains:** The pursuit of wealth can lead to decisions aimed at immediate financial benefits, sometimes at the expense of long-term ethical considerations. This might include engaging in unethical business practices, exploiting resources, or harming others.

- **Long-Term Values:** Spiritual and moral priorities typically emphasize long-term well-being, sustainable living, and the greater good. They advocate for decisions that, while perhaps not immediately profitable, contribute to the enduring health and harmony of individuals and communities.

2. **Ego and Self-Centrism vs. Humility and Service:**

- **Ego and Self-Centrism:** Wealth can foster a sense of superiority, entitlement, and self-centeredness. The desire for more can overshadow empathy and compassion, leading individuals to prioritize their success over the needs of others.

- **Humility and Service:** Many spiritual and moral traditions emphasize humility, compassion, and service to others. They teach that true fulfillment comes from helping others and contributing positively to society, rather than from accumulating personal wealth.

3. **Consequences of the Conflict:**

- **Stress and Dissatisfaction:** Constantly chasing wealth can lead to stress, anxiety, and a perpetual sense of dissatisfaction. When individuals tie their self-worth to their financial status they may never feel content, regardless of how much they acquire.

- **Loss of Meaning and Purpose:** Neglecting spiritual and moral priorities can result in a lack of deeper meaning and purpose in life. People may find that, despite their wealth, they feel empty and unfulfilled because they have not cultivated their inner life or contributed to something greater than themselves.

4. **Social Consequences:**

- **Inequality and Injustice:** The pursuit of wealth can exacerbate social inequalities as resources become concentrated in the hands of a few. This can lead to social unrest, crime, and a breakdown in social cohesion.

- **Environmental Degradation:** Prioritizing wealth over ethical considerations can result in the exploitation of natural resources, environmental degradation, and a disregard for sustainable practices. This not only harms the planet but also jeopardizes the well-being of future generations.

5. **Ethical Erosion:**

- **Compromised Integrity:** Individuals and organizations may compromise their integrity to achieve financial success. This can manifest as corruption, fraud, and unethical behavior, eroding trust within society.

- **Cultural Shifts:** A culture that prioritizes wealth can shift societal values, placing less importance on community, cooperation, and ethical conduct. This can lead to a more individualistic and competitive society, where collective well-being is undermined.

Balancing Wealth with Spiritual and Moral Priorities:

1. **Mindful Wealth Pursuit:** Individuals and organizations can strive to pursue wealth in a manner that aligns with their spiritual and moral values. This involves making ethical choices, prioritizing sustainability, and using wealth to benefit others.

2. **Integration of Values:** Encouraging a balance between material success and spiritual/moral growth can lead to a more holistic approach to life. This might include practices like philanthropy, ethical investing, and corporate social responsibility.

3. **Community and Support:** Fostering communities that support both material success and spiritual growth can help individuals navigate the tension between these priorities. Shared values and mutual support can reinforce the importance of balancing wealth with ethical and spiritual considerations.

In conclusion, while the pursuit of wealth can conflict with spiritual and moral priorities, it is possible to reconcile these aspects by integrating ethical considerations into the quest for financial success. This balance can lead to more fulfilling lives and healthier societies.

CHAPTER THREE

— Generosity and Giving —

In Acts 20:35, the apostle Paul quotes Jesus as saying, "It is more blessed to give than to receive." This statement encapsulates a profound truth about the nature of generosity and the blessings that come from selfless acts of giving.

1. **Joy of Generosity:** When we give to others, whether it's our time, resources, or love, we experience a sense of joy and fulfillment that transcends the satisfaction of receiving. Giving allows us to connect with others in meaningful ways, fostering a sense of community and belonging.

2. **Impact on Others:** Giving has the power to positively impact the lives of those in need. Whether it's providing material assistance to someone in poverty, offering emotional support to a friend in distress, or simply sharing a kind word or gesture, our acts of giving can bring comfort, hope, and encouragement to others.

3. **Cultivation of Virtues:** Generosity cultivates virtues such as compassion, empathy, and humility. When we give freely and willingly, we demonstrate a willingness to put the needs of others before our own, fostering a spirit of empathy and compassion that enriches our character.

4. **Spiritual Growth:** Giving is often associated with spiritual growth and development. Many religious

and philosophical traditions emphasize the importance of generosity as a pathway to spiritual enlightenment and fulfillment. By practicing generosity, we align ourselves with values of love, kindness, and service to others, deepening our spiritual connection and sense of purpose.

5. **Abundance Mindset:** Giving reflects an abundance mindset rather than a scarcity mindset. When we give freely, we operate from a belief that there is enough to go around and that our resources are meant to be shared for the greater good. This mindset fosters a sense of abundance, gratitude, and contentment in our lives.

6. **Reciprocity of Blessings.** Interestingly, the act of giving often leads to receiving blessings in return although not necessarily in the form of material wealth. When we give generously, we may experience blessings in the form of increased happiness, strengthened relationships, and a deeper sense of fulfillment and purpose in life.

Overall, the statement "it is more blessed to give than to receive" highlights the transformative power of generosity and the profound blessings that come from selflessly giving to others. By embracing a spirit of generosity in our lives, we not only enrich the lives of others but also experience abundant blessings and fulfillment ourselves.

In 2 Corinthians 9:7, the apostle Paul writes, "Each one must give as he has decided in his heart not reluctantly or under compulsion, for God loves a cheerful giver." This verse offers insight into the attitude and motivation behind giving, emphasizing the importance of cheerful generosity in the eyes of God.

1. **Heartfelt Giving:** The verse emphasizes that giving should be a voluntary and heartfelt act motivated by genuine compassion and generosity. It's not about giving out of obligation or pressure but about freely choosing to share one's resources with others out of a desire to help and bless them.

2. **Cheerful Attitude:** God values not only the act of giving but also the attitude with which it is done. A cheerful giver is someone who gives joyfully and eagerly, without hesitation or resentment. This cheerful attitude reflects a genuine love for others and a willingness to sacrificially give for their well-being.

3. **Reflection of God's Character:** The concept of cheerful giving aligns with the character of God, who is portrayed as a generous and loving provider throughout the Bible. Just as God gives abundantly and cheerfully to His creation, He delights in seeing His children emulate His generosity with cheerful hearts.

4. **Blessings of Giving:** Cheerful giving is often accompanied by blessings, both for the giver and the recipient. When we give cheerfully, we experience the joy and fulfillment that comes from making a positive difference in the lives of others. Additionally, God promises to bless those who give generously, multiplying their resources and providing for their needs.

5. **Expression of Faith:** Giving cheerfully is also an expression of faith and trust in God's provision. It demonstrates a belief that God will continue to supply all of our needs according to His riches and generosity, enabling us to give freely and joyfully without fear of lack.

6. **Impact on Others:** Cheerful giving has a positive impact not only on the giver but also on the recipients and the broader community. It spreads joy, hope, and kindness, fostering a sense of unity and solidarity as people come together to support and uplift one another.

In summary, 2 Corinthians 9:7 highlights the importance of cheerful generosity in the eyes of God. It encourages believers to give with joy and eagerness, out of a sincere desire to bless others and honor God with their resources. By embracing a spirit of cheerful giving, believers can experience the abundant blessings and fulfillment that come from aligning their hearts with God's generous and loving nature.

CHAPTER FOUR

— Poverty and Social Justice —

Communities in biblical times were instructed to treat the poor, widows, orphans, and foreigners with compassion, justice, and hospitality. Throughout the Old Testament, numerous passages outline specific instructions for caring for these vulnerable groups:

1. **The Poor:** In the Old Testament, various laws and commands emphasize the importance of generosity and compassion towards the poor. For example, the concept of gleaning allowed the poor to gather leftover crops from fields during harvest time (Leviticus 19:9-10. Deuteronomy 24:19-22). Additionally, the practice of giving alms and providing for the needs of the poor is encouraged throughout the Bible (Proverbs 19:17, Isaiah 58:7, Luke 12:33).

2. **Widows and Orphans:** Widows and orphans were considered among the most vulnerable members of society, often lacking the protection and support of a male provider. In numerous passages, God commands his people to defend the cause of widows and orphans and to ensure they receive justice and provision (Exodus 22:22-24, Deuteronomy 10:18, Psalm 146:9). The provision for widows and orphans extended to allowing them to glean in the fields and share in the communal feasts and offerings (Deuteronomy 14:28-29; 24:19-21).

3. **Foreigners:** The Old Testament also emphasizes hospitality and fair treatment towards foreigners or strangers living among the Israelites. God commands his people to love and show kindness to the foreigners, reminding them that they were once strangers in the land of Egypt (Exodus 22:21, Leviticus 19:34). Foreigners were to be included in communal celebrations and were entitled to justice and protection under the law (Deuteronomy 10:18-19; 24:17).

Overall, communities in biblical times were instructed to treat the poor, widows, orphans, and foreigners with kindness, justice, and hospitality. These vulnerable groups were not to be overlooked or marginalized but were to be included and cared for as integral members of the community. The principles of compassion and social justice outlined in the Old Testament continue to serve as a foundational guide for how individuals and communities should interact with and care for those in need today.

1. **Moral and Ethical Foundation:** For many people, the teachings of the Bible provide a moral and ethical foundation for their beliefs and actions. Within these teachings there is a clear emphasis on compassion, empathy, and justice, particularly for the marginalized and vulnerable in society. By focusing on these imperatives, individuals and communities can align their actions with deeply held religious values.

2. **Human Dignity and Worth:** The biblical imperative to support the poor and fight for justice is rooted in the belief that every individual is created in the image of God and therefore possesses inher-

ent dignity and worth. Recognizing and affirming the dignity of all people compels individuals to work towards ensuring that everyone has access to the resources and opportunities necessary for a dignified life.

3. **Social Responsibility:** The Bible consistently calls on individuals and communities to care for the poor, the oppressed, and the marginalized. This emphasis on social responsibility underscores the interconnectedness of humanity and highlights the importance of solidarity and collective action in addressing societal injustices.

4. **Addressing Structural Injustice:** The biblical imperative to fight for justice extends beyond acts of charity to include addressing systemic issues of injustice and inequality. By focusing on structural change, individuals and communities can work towards creating a more equitable society where the root causes of poverty and oppression are addressed.

5. **Building a Just Society:** Focusing on the biblical imperative to support the poor and fight for justice aligns with the vision of building a just and compassionate society. By actively working towards the well-being of all members of society, individuals and communities contribute to the creation of communities that reflect values of fairness, equality, and solidarity.

6. **Spiritual Fulfillment:** For many people of faith, engaging in acts of service, charity, and advocacy

by biblical teachings brings a sense of spiritual fulfillment and purpose. By living out their faith through actions that support the poor and promote justice, individuals experience a deeper connection to their religious beliefs and a greater sense of fulfillment in their lives.

— Biblical Calls for Justice —

In examining the biblical calls for justice, particularly focusing on the imperative to support the poor and fight for justice, one encounters a rich tapestry of teachings and principles throughout both the Old and New Testaments. Central to these teachings is the concept of righteousness, which encompasses not only personal morality but also social justice and care for the marginalized.

1. **Old Testament Perspective:**

- The Old Testament is replete with commands to care for the poor and marginalized. For instance, in the book of Leviticus, God commands the Israelites to leave part of their harvest for the poor and the foreigners (Leviticus 19: 9-10). This reflects a broader theme of concern for the vulnerable members of society.

- Prophets like Isaiah, Amos, and Micah repeatedly denounce injustice and oppression while advocating for the rights of the poor and marginalized. Isaiah 1:17 encapsulates this sentiment, urging people to "Learn to do right, seek justice. Defend the oppressed. Take up the cause of the fatherless, plead the case of the widow."

2. New Testament Perspective:

- Jesus himself emphasized the importance of caring for the marginalized. In the famous parable of the sheep and the goats (Matthew 25:31-46), Jesus equates caring for the hungry, thirsty, stranger, naked, sick, and imprisoned with serving him directly.

- The early Christian community also demonstrated a commitment to economic justice by sharing resources and caring for those in need (Acts 2:44-45; 4:32-35).

3. Justice as Integral to Righteousness:

- Throughout the Bible, justice is portrayed as integral to righteousness. Psalm 89:14 declares, "Righteousness and justice are the foundation of Your throne; love and faithfulness go before You." This linkage suggests that true righteousness includes seeking justice for all.

- Moreover, the biblical concept of justice extends beyond mere legalism to encompass the restoration of relationships and the establishment of right order in society.

4. Implications for Modern Society:

- These biblical teachings have profound implications for modern society. They call on Christians to advocate for policies and practices that address systemic injustices, such as poverty, inequality, and discrimination.

- Moreover, they challenge individuals to examine their actions and attitudes towards the poor and marginalized, encouraging acts of compassion, generosity, and solidarity.

Proverbs 31:19 is part of the passage commonly known as the Virtuous Woman or Wife of Noble Character. In this verse, it says: "She opens her arms to the poor and extends her hands to the needy."

This verse emphasizes the compassionate and proactive nature of the virtuous woman, highlighting her willingness to reach out and assist those who are poor and in need. However, while the verse itself doesn't directly mention speaking up or judging fairly, the broader context of the passage and the principles of justice and righteousness throughout the book of Proverbs shed light on how advocating for the rights of the poor and needy should be approached.

In the context of Proverbs as a whole, advocating for the rights of the poor and needy involves several key principles:

1. **Speaking Up:** The book of Proverbs contains numerous exhortations to speak up for those who cannot speak for themselves and to defend the rights of the poor and oppressed (Proverbs 31:8-9). This involves using one's voice and influence to advocate for justice and fairness on behalf of those who are marginalized or mistreated.

2. **Judging Fairly:** Proverbs emphasizes the importance of fair and impartial judgment, particularly

in cases involving the poor and needy. Judges and leaders are admonished to avoid showing partiality or favoritism and to administer justice with integrity and equity (Proverbs 24:23; 28:21). This principle underscores the importance of ensuring that the rights of the poor are protected and upheld in legal and societal contexts.

3. **Defending Rights:** Proverbs encourages individuals to actively defend the rights and interests of the poor and needy, particularly against exploitation and injustice. This includes speaking out against oppression, advocating for policy changes that promote social injustice, and providing practical assistance and support to those in need (Proverbs 14:31; 22:22-23).

In summary, while Proverbs 31:19 specifically highlights the compassionate actions of the virtuous woman towards the poor and needy, the broader principles of justice, fairness, and advocacy for the marginalized found throughout the book of Proverbs underscore the importance of speaking up and judging fairly in defending the rights of the poor and needy.

James 2:5 states, "Listen, my dear brothers and sisters: Has not God chosen those who are poor in the eyes of the world to be rich in faith and to inherit the kingdom He promised those who love him?"

This verse from the Epistle of James offers profound insights into the spiritual status of the poor in the kingdom of God and has significant implications for Christian perspectives on wealth and poverty.

1. **Rich in Faith:** James highlights that those who are poor in material wealth are often rich in faith. This challenges conventional notions of wealth and prosperity, emphasizing that true riches lie in one's relationship with God rather than in material possessions. It suggests that poverty does not equate to spiritual impoverishment and underscores the value of faith as a source of true abundance.

2. **Inheritance of the Kingdom:** The verse also affirms the promise that God has chosen the poor to inherit His kingdom. This emphasizes the inclusive nature of God's Kingdom, where status and wealth hold no significance. It suggests that in God's eyes, the worth of an individual is not determined by worldly measures but by their love for Him and their faithfulness.

3. **Implications for Christian Perspectives on Wealth and Poverty:** James' teaching challenges Christians to reconsider their perspectives on wealth and poverty. It calls for a shift away from the idolization of material wealth and success towards a deeper recognition of the value of spiritual riches and the dignity of all individuals regardless of their socioeconomic status.

These scriptures can inform both social policies and individual actions toward poverty alleviation in several ways:

1. **Social Policies:** By drawing on the principles and values found in these scriptures, policymakers can develop and implement social policies that prioritize the needs of the poor and marginalized. This may involve:

- **Economic Justice:** Implementing policies that address systemic issues of poverty and inequality, such as living wage laws, progressive taxation, and fair labor practices.

- **Social Safety Nets:** Establishing and strengthening social safety net programs, such as food assistance, affordable housing initiatives, and healthcare access, to ensure that all individuals have access to basic necessities.

- **Education and Training:** Investing in education and job training programs that empower individuals to break the cycle of poverty and achieve economic self-sufficiency.

- **Access to Healthcare:** Expanding access to affordable healthcare services, including preventive care and mental health support to address the healthcare needs of the poor and vulnerable.

- **Criminal Justice Reform:** Implementing reforms to address systemic injustices within the criminal justice system, such as ending mass incarceration and promoting alternatives to punitive measures for nonviolent offenses.

2. **Individual Actions:** Individually people can also be guided by these scriptures to take practical actions to alleviate poverty in their communities. This may include:

- **Charitable Giving:** Supporting organizations and initiatives that work to alleviate poverty and empower the poor through financial donations, volunteerism, and fundraising efforts.

- **Advocacy and Activism:** Advocating for policy changes that address the root causes of poverty and promote social justice through letter-writing campaigns, grassroots organizing, and participation in advocacy groups.

- **Community Engagement:** Getting involved in local community initiatives and programs that provide support and resources to the poor and marginalized, such as food banks, homeless shelters, and job training programs.

- **Education and Awareness:** Raising awareness about issues of poverty and inequality within one's social circles and communities, and educating others about the biblical principles and values that inform efforts to address these issues.

- **Building Relationships:** Building meaningful relationships with individuals who are experiencing poverty, offering practical assistance, emotional support, and spiritual encouragement, and advocating for their dignity and rights.

By integrating these scriptures into both social policies and individual actions, communities can work towards a more just and compassionate society where all individuals have the opportunity to thrive and flourish, regardless of their socioeconomic status.

Application to Modern Life:

Here are some contemporary examples of churches and Christian organizations effectively addressing poverty and promoting justice:

1. **Faith-Based Community Development Initiatives:** Organizations like Habitat for Humanity and World Vision engage in community development projects worldwide, providing housing, clean water, education, and economic opportunities to impoverished communities.

2. **Soup Kitchens and Food Banks:** Many churches operate soup kitchens and food banks to provide meals and groceries to individuals and families experiencing food insecurity. These initiatives offer immediate relief to those in need while also addressing underlying issues of poverty and hunger.

3. **Microfinance and Entrepreneurship Programs:** Christian organizations such as Opportunity International and Kiva provide microloans and business training to individuals in developing countries, enabling them to start or expand small businesses and lift themselves out of poverty.

4. **Advocacy and Policy Reform:** Churches and Christian organizations often advocate for policy changes that address systemic issues of poverty and injustice. For example, organizations like Bread for the World and the National Association of Evangelicals advocate for policies that support hungry and poor people both domestically and internationally.

5. **International Relief and Development:** Christian humanitarian organizations like Samaritan's Purse and World Relief provide emergency relief and long-term development assistance to communities affected by poverty, natural disasters, and conflict. They offer services such as healthcare, education, and vocational training to help individuals rebuild their lives and communities.

6. **Prison Ministries and Criminal Justice Reform:** Churches and Christian organizations engage in prison ministries to support incarcerated individuals and their families, offering spiritual guidance, rehabilitation programs, and reentry assistance. Additionally, these groups advocate for criminal justice reform policies that prioritize rehabilitation and alternatives to incarceration.

7. **Homelessness Prevention and Housing Assistance:** Churches often collaborate with local governments and nonprofits to provide housing assistance and support services to individuals and families experiencing homelessness. Some churches also offer transitional housing programs and supportive services to help people transition out of homelessness and regain stability in their lives.

These examples demonstrate the diverse ways in which churches and Christian organizations are actively engaged in addressing poverty and promoting justice both locally and globally. Through their efforts, they embody the teachings of Jesus Christ and work towards building a more equitable and compassionate society for all.

Here are some practical suggestions for readers to engage in social justice within their communities:

1. **Educate Yourself:** Take the time to learn about social justice issues affecting your community and beyond. Read books, watch documentaries, and engage with diverse perspectives to deepen your understanding of these issues.

2. **Listen and Learn from Others:** Listen to the experiences and perspectives of people directly affected by social injustices. Engage in conversations with individuals from different backgrounds and communities to gain insight into their lived experiences.

3. **Volunteer:** Get involved with local organizations and initiatives that address social justice issues. Volunteer your time and skills to support efforts related to poverty alleviation, racial justice, environmental sustainability, LGBTQ + rights, and other causes.

4. **Advocate for Change:** Use your voice to advocate for policy changes and systemic reforms that promote social justice. Write letters to elected officials, participate in rallies and protests, and support advocacy campaigns organized by grassroots movements and advocacy groups.

5. **Support Ethical Businesses:** Choose to support businesses that prioritize ethical practices, fair labor standards, environmental sustainability, and social responsibility. Consider shopping locally and

purchasing from companies that are committed to making a positive impact in their communities.

6. **Engage in Dialogue and Bridge Building:** Foster open and respectful dialogue with individuals who may hold different viewpoints or backgrounds. Seek common ground and work towards building bridges of understanding and empathy across divides.

7. **Address Bias and Discrimination:** Challenge bias and discrimination whenever you encounter it, whether it's in your workplace, community, or social circles. Stand up against racism, sexism, homophobia, transphobia, ableism, and other forms of discrimination, and strive to create inclusive and welcoming environments for all.

8. **Support Marginalized Communities:** Stand in solidarity with marginalized communities and amplify their voices and concerns. Support organizations led by and serving marginalized populations, and advocate for their rights and dignity.

9. **Practice Allyship:** Be an ally to marginalized individuals and communities by actively listening, learning, and taking action to support their struggles for justice and equality. Use your privilege and influence to advocate for those who may not have the same opportunities and access to resources.

10. **Continue Learning and Growing:** Social justice is an ongoing journey, and it's important to continually educate yourself, reflect on your own biases

and privileges, and seek opportunities for personal growth and development in your understanding and commitment to social justice.

By taking these practical steps, readers can actively contribute to creating positive change and promoting social justice within their communities and beyond.

CHAPTER FIVE

— Stewardship and Management —

This section delves into the concept of stewardship as a fundamental aspect of biblical teachings on wealth. It explains how being a good steward not only involves managing one's finances wisely but also encompasses a broader ethical responsibility to use resources in a manner that honors God.

The concept of stewardship in the biblical context is deeply rooted in the understanding that everything ultimately belongs to God, and humans are entrusted with the responsibility of managing and caring for God's creation. Here are some key principles of biblical stewardship:

1. **Ownership Belongs to God:** The Bible teaches that God is the creator and owner of all things (Psalm 24:1). As stewards, humans are called to recognize that everything they have—time, talents, resources, and the earth itself—is a gift from God.

2. **Responsibility to Care for Creation:** Stewardship involves caring for and responsibly managing the earth and its resources. This includes protecting the environment, conserving natural resources, and promoting sustainability (Genesis 2:15).

3. **Accountability:** Stewards are accountable to God for how they manage the resources entrusted to them. In the parable of the talents (Matthew 25:14-30), Jesus teaches that individuals will be held

accountable for how they use the talents and resources they have been given.

4. **Integrity and Faithfulness:** Stewards are called to manage resources with integrity, honesty, and faithfulness. This involves using resources wisely, avoiding waste and extravagance, and seeking to honor God in all aspects of life (Luke 46: 10-12).

5. **Generosity and Sharing:** Stewardship involves a spirit of generosity and sharing with others, especially those in need. The Bible encourages believers to give generously, share with the poor, and support the work of the church and ministry (2 Corinthians 9:6-7, Acts 2:44-45).

6. **Investment in Kingdom Purposes:** Stewardship includes investing time, talents, and resources in advancing the kingdom of God. This may involve supporting missions and evangelism, serving others in love, and using one's gifts to glorify God and serve others (Matthew 6:33).

7. **Multiplication and Growth:** Stewards are called to multiply and grow the resources entrusted to them for the glory of God and the benefit of others. This may involve investing in personal and spiritual growth, developing talents and skills, and seeking opportunities to make a positive impact in the world (Matthew 25: 20-21).

8. **Humility and Gratitude:** Stewardship is rooted in humility and gratitude, recognizing that all blessings come from God. Stewards are called to

approach life with a spirit of humility, acknowledging their dependence on God and expressing gratitude for His provision (1 Chronicles 29: 14-16).

In summary, the concept of stewardship in the biblical context emphasizes recognizing God's ownership, responsibly managing resources, being accountable to God, living with integrity and faithfulness, practicing generosity and sharing, investing in kingdom purposes, seeking growth and multiplication, and living with humility and gratitude. By embracing these principles, individuals can honor God as faithful stewards of His creation.

The Concept of Stewardship as Managing God's Resources:

In Matthew 25:21, Jesus tells the parable of the talents, in which a master entrusts his servants with different amounts of money (talents) before going away on a journey. When he returns he assesses how each servant has managed the resources he entrusted to them. The servant who had received five talents had invested them and earned five more talents, and his master commends him saying, "Well done, good and faithful servant! You have been faithful with a few things; I will put you in charge of many things. Come and share your master's happiness!"

In this parable, the talents represent the resources and abilities that God entrusts to each person. While talents could represent various aspects of life, including skills, opportunities, wealth, and spiritual gifts, they ultimately symbolize the resources and blessings that God bestows upon His people.

The principle illustrated in this parable is that God expects His followers to use their gifts and resources wisely and productively for His kingdom's purposes. The servant who faithfully invested his talents and produced a return was commended and rewarded by his master. Conversely, the servant who buried his talent out of fear and failed to make any profit faced judgment.

This parable teaches several important principles about stewardship:

1. **Responsibility:** God entrusts His followers with resources and abilities, expecting them to use them wisely and productively.

2. **Accountability:** God holds His followers accountable for how they manage the resources He has given them. He expects them to be faithful stewards who invest in His kingdom and bear fruit.

3. **Reward:** Faithful stewardship is rewarded with greater responsibility and participation in God's joy and blessings.

4. **Risk-taking and Initiative:** The parable encourages believers to take risks and use their talents boldly for God's purposes, rather than fearfully burying them out of caution.

Ultimately, Matthew 25:21 underscores the importance of faithful stewardship and the expectation that God's resources will be used to advance His kingdom and bring glory to Him. It challenges believers to be proactive, creative, and diligent in using their talents and resources for God's purposes, knowing that they will be held accountable for how they have invested them.

In Luke 16:10-11, Jesus speaks about the faithful management of resources, saying:

"Whoever can be trusted with very little can also be trusted with much, and whoever is dishonest with very little will also be dishonest with much. So if you have not been trustworthy in handling worldly wealth, who will trust you with true riches?"

In this passage, Jesus emphasizes the principle of stewardship and the importance of faithful management of resources, particularly worldly wealth. Here's a breakdown of the key points:

1. **Trustworthiness and Responsibility:** Jesus begins by highlighting the principle that faithfulness in small matters leads to greater responsibilities. If someone proves trustworthy with small amounts of wealth or resources, they can be entrusted with larger responsibilities. This underscores the idea that how we handle even the smallest resources reflects our character and trustworthiness.

2. **Dishonesty and Lack of Trust:** Conversely, Jesus warns against dishonesty and unfaithfulness in managing resources. If someone proves to be dishonest or untrustworthy with even small amounts, it raises questions about their reliability and integrity. A lack of trustworthiness in managing worldly wealth can lead to a loss of opportunities for greater responsibilities and blessings.

3. **True Riches:** Jesus contrasts worldly wealth with "true riches." While worldly wealth refers to material possessions and resources, true riches likely refer to spiritual blessings, eternal rewards, and the wealth of God's kingdom. Jesus suggests that faithful stewardship of worldly wealth is a prerequisite for receiving true riches from God.

4. **Understanding the Heart:** This passage goes beyond mere financial management and addresses the condition of the heart. Jesus is concerned with the motivations, attitudes, and priorities that underlie our stewardship of resources. Faithful stewardship is not just about external actions but about the state of the heart before God.

5. **Implications for Stewardship:** The principles Jesus teaches in these verses have profound implications for how believers approach stewardship. It challenges us to examine our attitudes towards wealth and possessions, to prioritize faithfulness and integrity in managing resources, and to recognize that our stewardship has spiritual significance and eternal consequences.

In summary, Luke 16:10-11 underscores the importance of faithful stewardship of resources, highlights the relationship between trustworthiness and responsibility, warns against dishonesty and lack of trust, and points to the true riches of God's kingdom that await those who are faithful in managing worldly wealth.

Managing resources wisely involves several key principles:

1. **Budgeting and Financial Planning:** Wisely managing wealth requires careful budgeting and financial planning. This involves creating a budget, tracking expenses, and setting financial goals to ensure that resources are used effectively and responsibly (Proverbs 21:5).

2. **Living Within Means:** Managing resources wisely means living within one's means and avoiding excessive spending or debt. This may require making sacrifices and prioritizing needs over wants to ensure financial stability and security (Proverbs 22:7).

3. **Diversification and Risk Management:** Wise stewardship of wealth involves diversifying investments and managing risk. This may include investing in a variety of assets and industries to spread risk, as well as having appropriate insurance and contingency plans in place (Ecclesiastes 11:2).

4. **Seeking Wise Counsel:** It is important to seek wise counsel and advice from trusted advisors when making financial decisions. This may involve consulting with financial planners, accountants, and other professionals who can provide guidance and expertise (Proverbs 15:22).

5. **Evaluating Motivations:** Managing resources wisely also involves evaluating one's motivations and priorities. Individuals should examine their hearts and ensure that their financial decisions are

aligned with God's purposes and values (Matthew 6:24).

Ultimately, managing resources wisely requires a combination of financial prudence, ethical principles, and spiritual discernment. By recognizing the responsibilities that come with wealth and adhering to biblical principles of stewardship, individuals can use their wealth to honor God and bless others.

CHAPTER SIX

— Trust, Contentment, and Providence —

In Matthew 6:24, Jesus teaches, "No one can serve two masters. Either you will hate the one and love the other, or you will be devoted to the one and despise the other. You cannot serve both God and money."

This verse highlights the inherent conflict between serving God and serving material wealth. Here's a breakdown of the key concepts:

1. **Serving Two Masters:** Jesus uses the metaphor of serving two masters to illustrate the impossibility of simultaneously devoting oneself to both God and money. Serving a master implies complete loyalty, obedience, and devotion. However, trying to serve both God and money leads to divided loyalty and conflicting priorities.

2. **Love and Devotion:** Jesus contrasts the concepts of love and devotion, emphasizing that one's affections and allegiance cannot be divided between God and material wealth. True devotion to God requires exclusive love and commitment, which cannot coexist with a devotion to money and worldly possessions.

3. **Prioritizing God:** The verse underscores the importance of prioritizing God above all else. Jesus teaches elsewhere that the greatest commandment is to love the Lord your God with all your heart, soul,

mind, and strength (Mark 12:30). Serving God as the primary master means aligning one's life and values with His kingdom and purposes.

4. **Consequences of Dual Service:** Jesus warns of the consequences of attempting to serve both God and money. Divided loyalty leads to inner conflict, dissatisfaction, and spiritual unrest. It also results in a distorted perspective on life, where material wealth becomes the primary focus and source of security, rather than God.

5. **Implications for Contentment and Trust:** Serving God exclusively cultivates contentment and trust in His providence. Contentment arises from finding satisfaction and fulfillment in God alone, rather than in material possessions of wealth (Philippians 4:11-13). Trust in God's providence involves relying on Him for provision and guidance, rather than placing confidence in earthly riches (Proverbs 3:5-6).

Matthew 6:24 teaches that it is impossible to serve both God and money simultaneously. It emphasizes the importance of prioritizing God above material wealth, cultivating contentment and trust in His providence, and recognizing the inherent conflict between devotion to God and devotion to worldly possessions. By choosing to serve God as the primary master, individuals can experience true fulfillment, peace, and security in Him.

In Philippians 4:19, the apostle Paul writes, "And my God will meet all your needs according to the riches of His glory in Christ Jesus." This verse provides reassurance and encouragement to believers, affirming God's faithfulness in meeting their needs. Here's a deeper look at the key concepts:

1. **God's Provision:** The verse begins with the assurance that " my God will meet all your needs." This highlights the personal relationship believers have with God and His active involvement in providing for them. It emphasizes that God is not distant or indifferent but intimately concerned with the well-being of His people.

2. **Comprehensive Care:** The promise extends to "all your needs," encompassing every aspect of life— physical, emotional, spiritual, and relational. God's provision is not limited to material necessities but includes everything necessary for abundant life and flourishing in Christ.

3. **Source of Provision:** The verse emphasizes that God's provision is sourced in "the riches of His glory in Christ Jesus." This points to the abundance and sufficiency of God's resources, which are inexhaustible and boundless. God's provision flows from His glory, reflecting His character of goodness, generosity, and abundance.

4. **In Christ Jesus:** The provision of God is intimately connected to the person and work of Jesus Christ. Believers are united with Christ through faith, and all blessings and provisions come through Him. It is in Christ that believers experience the fullness of God's provision and grace (Ephesians 1:3).

5. **Assurance of Faith:** The promise of God's provision is grounded in faith and trust in Him. As believers entrust their needs to God and rely on His faithfulness, they can have confidence that He will fulfill His promises and meet them at their point of need.

6. **Riches of His Glory:** The phrase "the riches of His glory" emphasizes the immeasurable abundance and splendor of God's resources. God's provision is not limited by human constraints but flows from His infinite wealth and majesty.

Philippians 4:19 assures believers that God will meet all their needs according to His abundant riches in Christ Jesus. This promise provides comfort, encouragement, and a foundation for trust in God's faithfulness and provision in every circumstance of life.

Finding contentment and trusting in God's provision are essential aspects of the Christian faith that involve both practical and spiritual dimensions. Here's a discussion on how Christians can find contentment and what it means to trust in God's provision.

1. **Cultivating a Grateful Heart:** Contentment often begins with gratitude. Christians can cultivate contentment by intentionally focusing on the blessings and provisions that God has already provided in their lives. Practicing gratitude helps shift the focus from what is lacking to what has been given, fostering a sense of satisfaction and fulfillment (1 Thessalonians 5:18).

2. **Aligning Desires with God's Will:** Contentment involves aligning one's desires with God's will and purposes. This means seeking first the kingdom of God and His righteousness, rather than pursuing worldly ambitions or material possessions (Matthew 6:33). By prioritizing spiritual values and eternal blessings, Christians can experience a deeper sense of contentment that transcends earthly circumstances.

3. **Letting Go of Comparison:** Comparing oneself to others often leads to dissatisfaction and discontentment. Christians can find contentment by embracing their unique identity and calling in Christ, recognizing that God has a unique plan and purpose for each individual (Galatians 6:4-5). Instead of comparing themselves to others, believers can focus on fulfilling God's purpose for their own lives.

4. **Trusting in God's Timing:** Trusting in God's provision involves surrendering control and trusting in His timing and wisdom. This means acknowledging that God knows what is best for His children and will provide for their needs in His perfect timing (Psalm 37:5). Trusting in God's timing requires patience, faith, and a willingness to wait for His provision to unfold.

5. **Relying on God's Promises:** Christians can find assurance and confidence in God's promises regarding provision and care. Scripture is replete with promises that God will provide for His people, meet their needs, and never forsake them (Matthew 6:25-34, Hebrews 13: 5-6). By anchoring their faith in

God's promises, believers can trust in His provision even in uncertainty and difficulty.

6. **Seeking Spiritual Fulfillment:** Contentment ultimately comes from a deep and abiding relationship with God. Christians can find contentment by seeking satisfaction and fulfillment in spiritual pursuits such as prayer and worship, scripture study and serving others (Philippians 4:11-13). By nurturing their relationship with God, believers can experience a lasting sense of contentment that transcends circumstances.

7. **Practicing Detachment from Materialism:** Material possessions and worldly wealth often promise happiness but ultimately leave people feeling empty and unsatisfied. Christians can find contentment by practicing detachment from materialism and placing their trust in God rather than in earthly riches (1 Timothy 6:6-10). By prioritizing spiritual treasures over material possessions, believers can experience true contentment and fulfillment in Christ.

Finding contentment and trusting God's provision involves cultivating gratitude, aligning desires with God's will, letting go of comparisons, trusting in God's timing and promises, seeking spiritual fulfillment, and practicing detachment from materialism. By embracing these principles, Christians can experience a deeper sense of contentment and trust in God's faithful provision in every area of life.

CHAPTER SEVEN

— Application to Modern Life —

Ancient wisdom from Matthew 6:24 and Philippians 4:19 offers valuable insights that can be applied to contemporary financial challenges in several ways:

1. **Prioritizing Values Over Materialism:** In a consumer-driven society where material wealth often takes precedence, the teachings of Matthew 6:24 remind us of the importance of prioritizing spiritual values over materialism. By recognizing that true fulfillment comes from serving God rather than money, individuals can resist the pressures of consumer culture and make decisions that align with their values and beliefs.

2. **Balancing Work and Faith:** In today's fast-paced world, many people struggle to find a balance between work and faith. Matthew 6:24 challenges us to consider whether our work serves as a means of worshiping God or merely pursuing material gain. By integrating our faith into our work and striving to honor God in all that we do, we can find greater purpose and satisfaction in our careers.

3. **Managing Financial Stress:** Philippians 4:19 reassures believers that God will meet all their needs according to His riches in Christ Jesus. This promise offers comfort and hope to those facing financial stress or uncertainty. By trusting in God's provision and seeking His guidance in financial matters,

individuals can find peace and security amid financial challenges.

4. **Cultivating Contentment:** In a culture that often promotes discontentment and consumerism, the concept of contentment found in Philippians 4:19 offers a powerful antidote. By practicing gratitude for what we have and finding satisfaction in God's provision, we can resist the temptation to constantly strive for more and instead experience true contentment in every circumstance.

5. **Living Within Means:** Both passages emphasize the importance of living within our means and avoiding excessive pursuit of wealth. By practicing financial stewardship and prioritizing needs over wants, individuals can avoid the pitfalls of debt and overspending, leading to greater financial stability and freedom.

6. **Sharing Resources with Others:** Philippians 4:19 reminds us of God's abundant provision, not just for ourselves but also for others. By embracing a spirit of generosity and sharing our resources with those in need, we can live out the principles of stewardship and compassion taught in Scripture, making a positive impact in the lives of others and advancing God's kingdom on earth.

In conclusion, the ancient wisdom found in Matthew 6:24 and Philippians 4:19 offers timeless principles that are highly relevant to contemporary financial challenges. By applying these teachings to our lives, we can navigate financial decisions with wisdom and faith, finding contentment, peace, and security in God's provision.

Call to Action

I encourage readers to reflect on their personal and communal financial practices in light of biblical teachings that can be an empowering call to action. Here are some ways to inspire reflection and action:

1. **Personal Reflection:** I encourage readers to set aside time for personal reflection and introspection and to examine their financial habits, priorities, and attitudes towards money in light of biblical principles. I suggest journaling prompts or guided questions to help you explore your relationship with money and God's teachings on stewardship.

2. **Study and Discussion Groups:** I encourage readers to participate in study and discussion groups focused on biblical teachings on finance and stewardship. These groups can provide opportunities for shared learning, accountability, and support as individuals seek to align their financial practices with biblical principles. You can provide resources, such as study guides or recommended readings to facilitate group discussions.

3. **Practical Application:** I encourage readers to take practical steps towards aligning their financial practices with biblical teachings. This could include creating a budget based on biblical principles of stewardship, setting financial goals that reflect kingdom priorities, and actively seeking opportunities for generosity and stewardship in their daily lives.

4. **Seeking Wise Counsel:** I encourage readers to seek wise counsel and guidance from trusted mentors, financial advisors, or pastors. I encourage them to be open to feedback and advice as they seek to make changes to their financial practices in line with biblical teachings.

5. **Community Engagement:** I encourage readers to engage with their communities and churches in conversations about financial stewardship and generosity. I encourage them to participate in initiatives focused on financial education, debt reduction, and poverty alleviation within their communities.

6. **Accountability Partnerships:** I encourage readers to form accountability partnerships with friends or family members who share their desire to align their financial practices with biblical principles. These partnerships can provide encouragement, support, and accountability as individuals seek to make positive changes in their financial lives.

7. **Continual Reflection and Growth:** I encourage readers to view financial stewardship as an ongoing journey of growth and transformation. I encourage them to regularly revisit their financial practices, reflect on their progress, and seek opportunities for further growth and alignment with biblical principles.

While encouraging readers to reflect on their personal and communal financial practices in light of biblical teachings, they are empowered to take meaningful steps towards financial stewardship, generosity, and alignment with God's purposes for their lives.

Below are some study questions for each section that will encourage deeper reflection and group discussion related to Matthew 6:24 and Philippians 4:19

Section 1: Understanding the Text

1. What does Matthew 6:24 teach us about the relationship between serving God and serving money?

2. How does Philippians 4:19 assure believers of God's provision for their needs?

3. Reflect on a time when you felt torn between pursuing God's will and pursuing material wealth. How did you resolve this conflict?

Section 2: Spiritual Implications

1. How does prioritizing God over material wealth impact our daily decisions and lifestyle?

2. In what ways can trusting in God's provision strengthen our faith and reliance on Him?

3. Discuss examples from your own life or from scripture of individuals who demonstrated contentment despite challenging circumstances.

Section 3: Practical Application

1.   What are some practical steps we can take to align our financial practices with biblical principles?

2.   How can we cultivate contentment in a culture that often promotes discontentment and consumerism?

3.   Share examples of how you have experienced God's provision in your own life and how it has impacted your faith and trust in Him.

Section 4: Community Engagement

1.   How can our churches and communities promote financial stewardship and generosity among believers?

2.   Discuss the role of accountability and support in helping individuals align their financial practices with biblical principles.

3.   Brainstorm ideas for community initiatives or outreach programs focused on financial education and poverty alleviation.

— Bibliography —

Here are some suggestions for further readings and books for those interested in exploring more about biblical economics:

1. **Money, Possessions, and Eternity, by Randy Alcorn:** This comprehensive book explores the biblical perspective on money, possessions, and stewardship. Alcorn addresses topics such as generosity, contentment, and investing in eternal rewards.

2. **The Treasure Principle, by Randy Alcorn:** In this short but impactful book, Alcorn unpacks Jesus' teachings on money and stewardship, emphasizing the eternal significance of investing in God's kingdom.

3. **Generous Justice: How God's Grace Makes Us Just, by Timothy Keller:** Keller explores the biblical mandate for social justice and compassion towards the poor, drawing on both Old and New Testament teachings.

4. **The Economics of Neighborly Love: Investing in Your Community's Compassion and Capacity, by Tom Nelson:** Nelson offers a practical guide to applying biblical principles of economics and stewardship to community development and social justice efforts.

5. **For the Least of These: A Biblical Answer to Poverty, by Anne R. Bradley and Art Lindsley:** This book explores the biblical approach to poverty

alleviation, emphasizing the importance of compassion, empowerment, and holistic solutions.

6. **God and Money: How We Discovered True Riches at Harvard Business School, by John Cortines and Gregory Baumer:** Cortines and Baumer share their journey of discovering biblical wisdom on money and stewardship while attending Harvard Business School.

7. **Rich Christians in an Age of Hunger: Moving from Affluence to Generosity, by Ronald J. Sider:** Sider challenges affluent Christians to examine their lifestyles and priorities in light of the biblical call to generosity and compassion towards the poor.

8. **The Generosity Factor: Discover the Joy of Giving Your Time, Talent, and Treasure, by Ken Blanchard and S. Truett Cathy:** Blanchard and Cathy explore the transformative power of generosity and the joy that comes from giving of one's time, talent, and treasure.

9. **Money and Power: The History of Business, by Howard Means:** This historical overview traces the development of economic systems and business practices from ancient times to the present day, providing valuable insights into the intersection of economics and society.

10. **The Bible and Economics: A Critical Guide edited by Richard H. Gilmour and Leo D. Lefebure:** This scholarly collection of essays examines

the intersection of biblical studies and economics, offering diverse perspectives on topics such as wealth, poverty, and social justice.

These books provide a wealth of insights into biblical economics, stewardship, generosity, and social justice, offering valuable resources for individuals seeking to align their financial practices with biblical principles.

— About the Author —

Boyce N. Pearson is a retired public school music teacher. He taught in the Little Rock, Arkansas education system for 39 years. In his spare time, he taught the stock market game in the after-school programs and participated in numerous workshops with Economics Arkansas. His love for the children's ministry has led him to teach Bible classes for youth and economic workshops in various church ministries throughout the Arkansas region. For more than 15 years, Boyce has served on the Arkansas Credit Union's credit committee and board of directors.